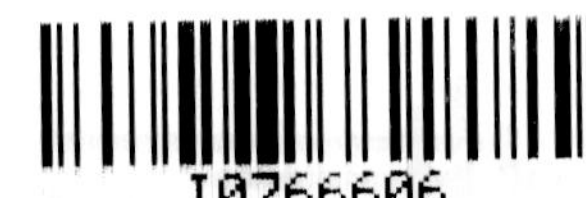

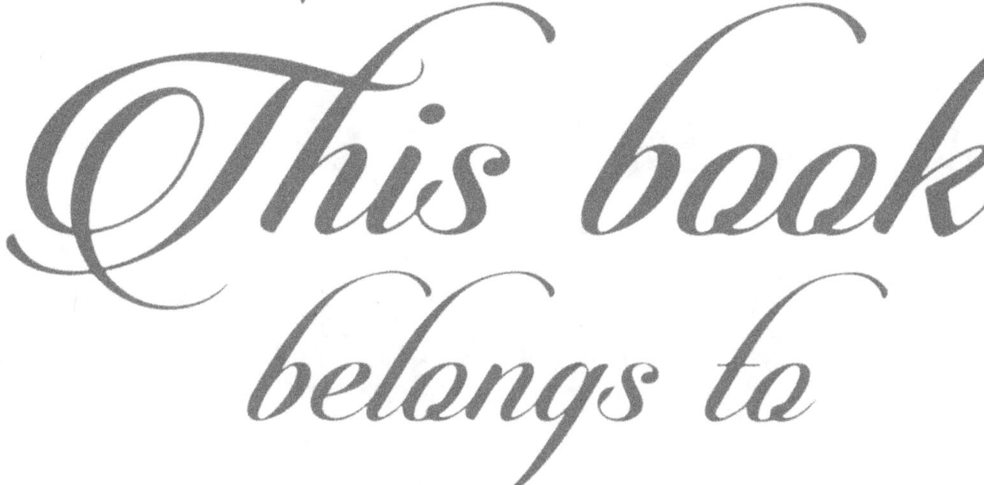

This book
belongs to

....

....

....

....

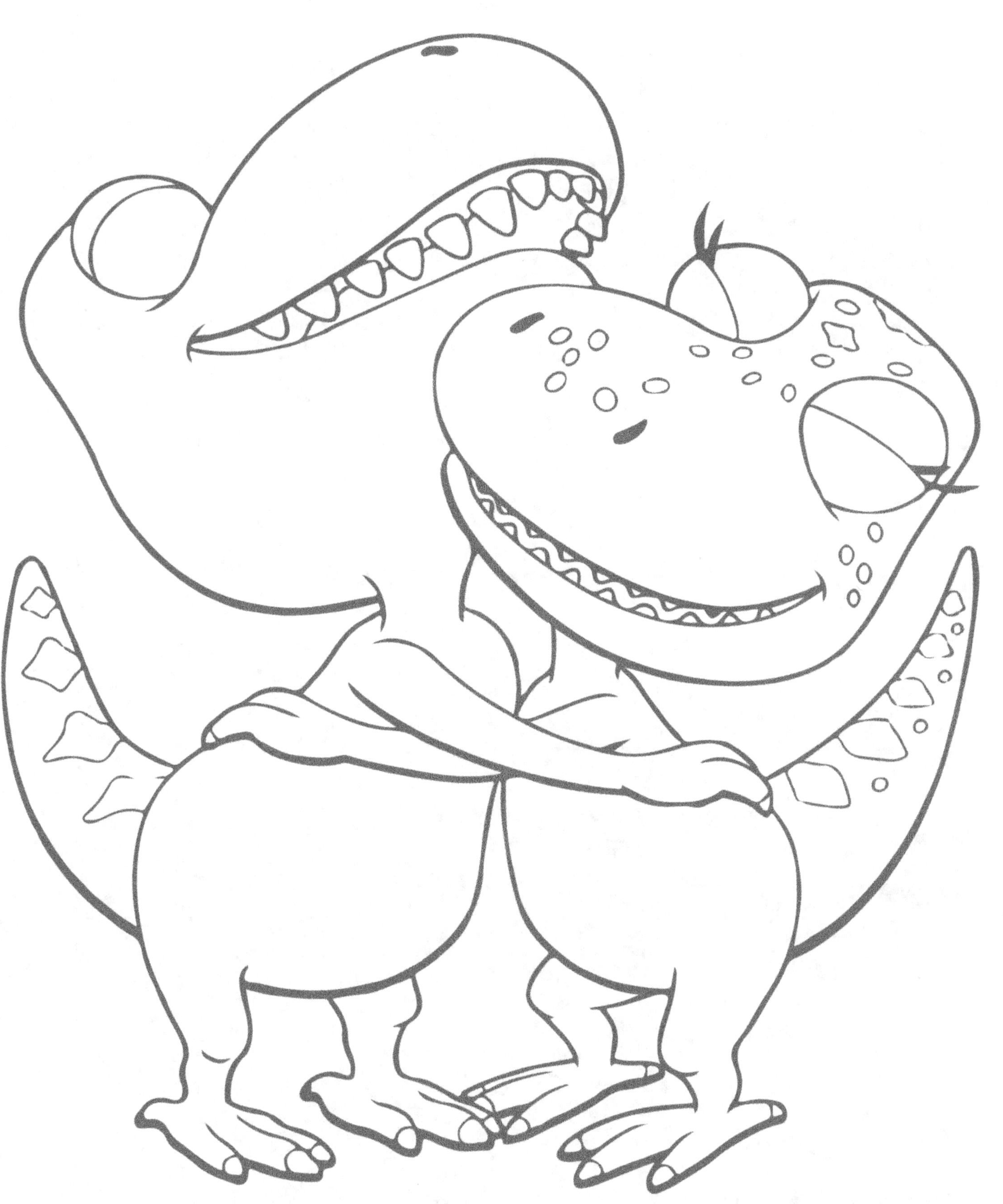

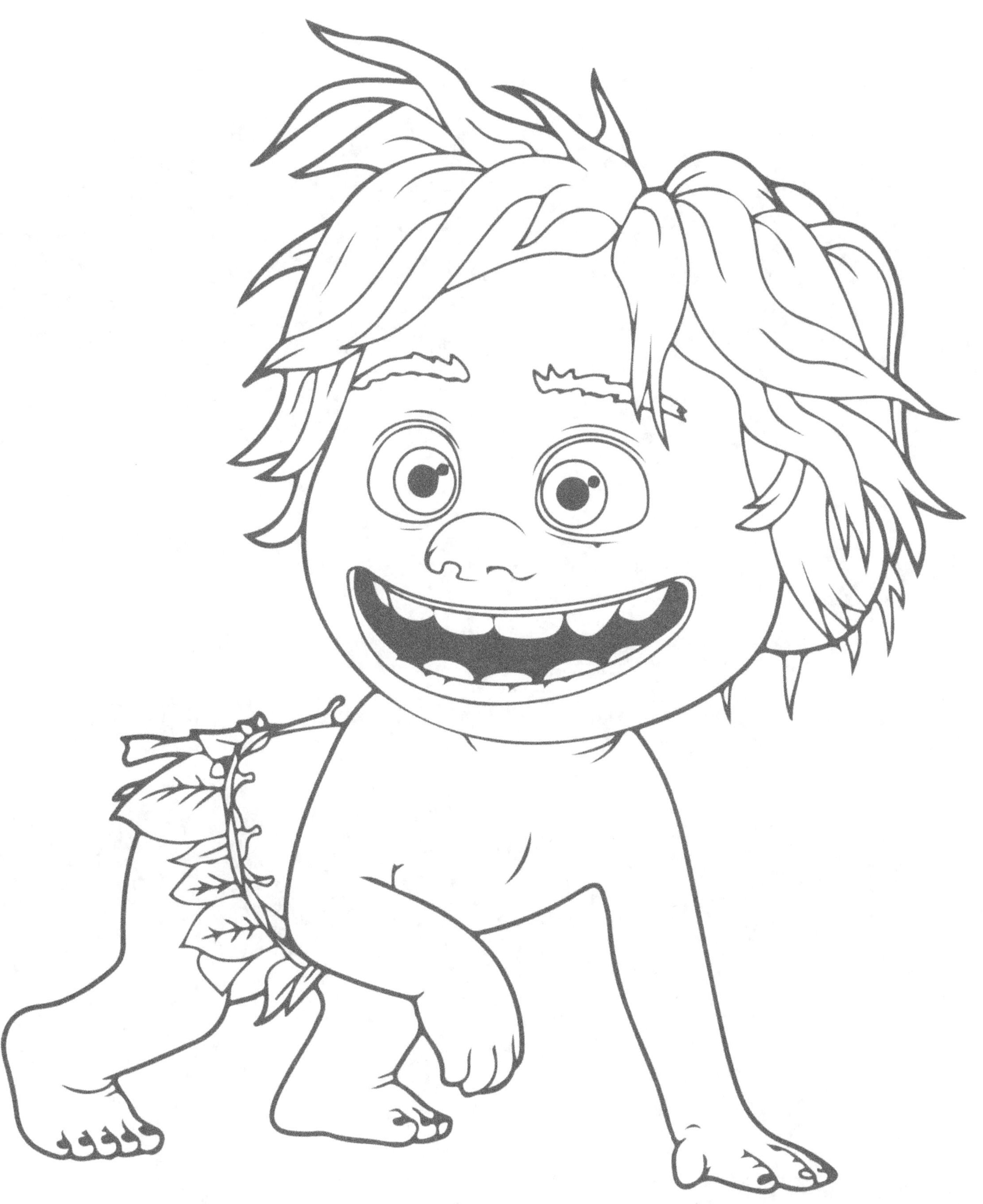

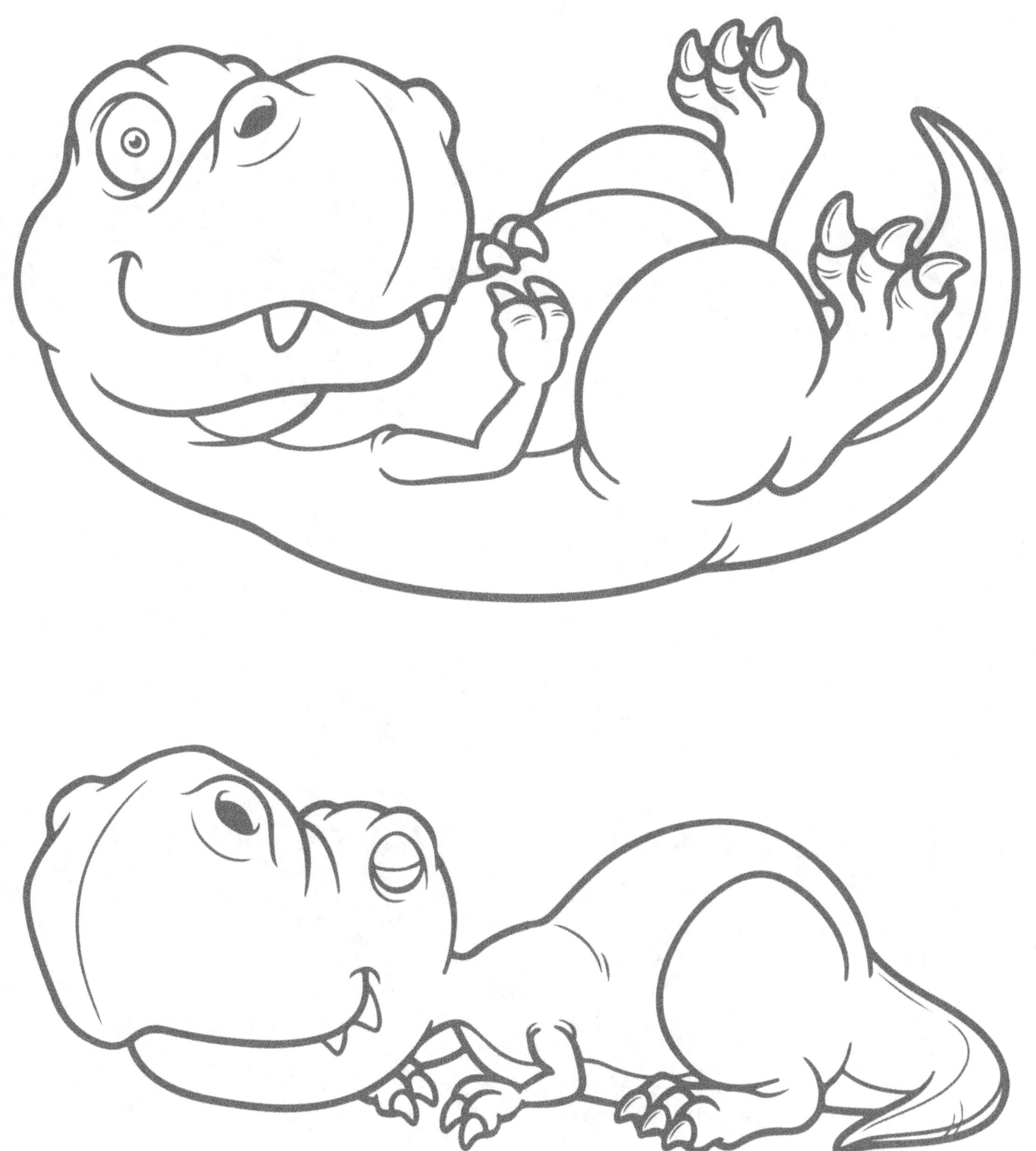

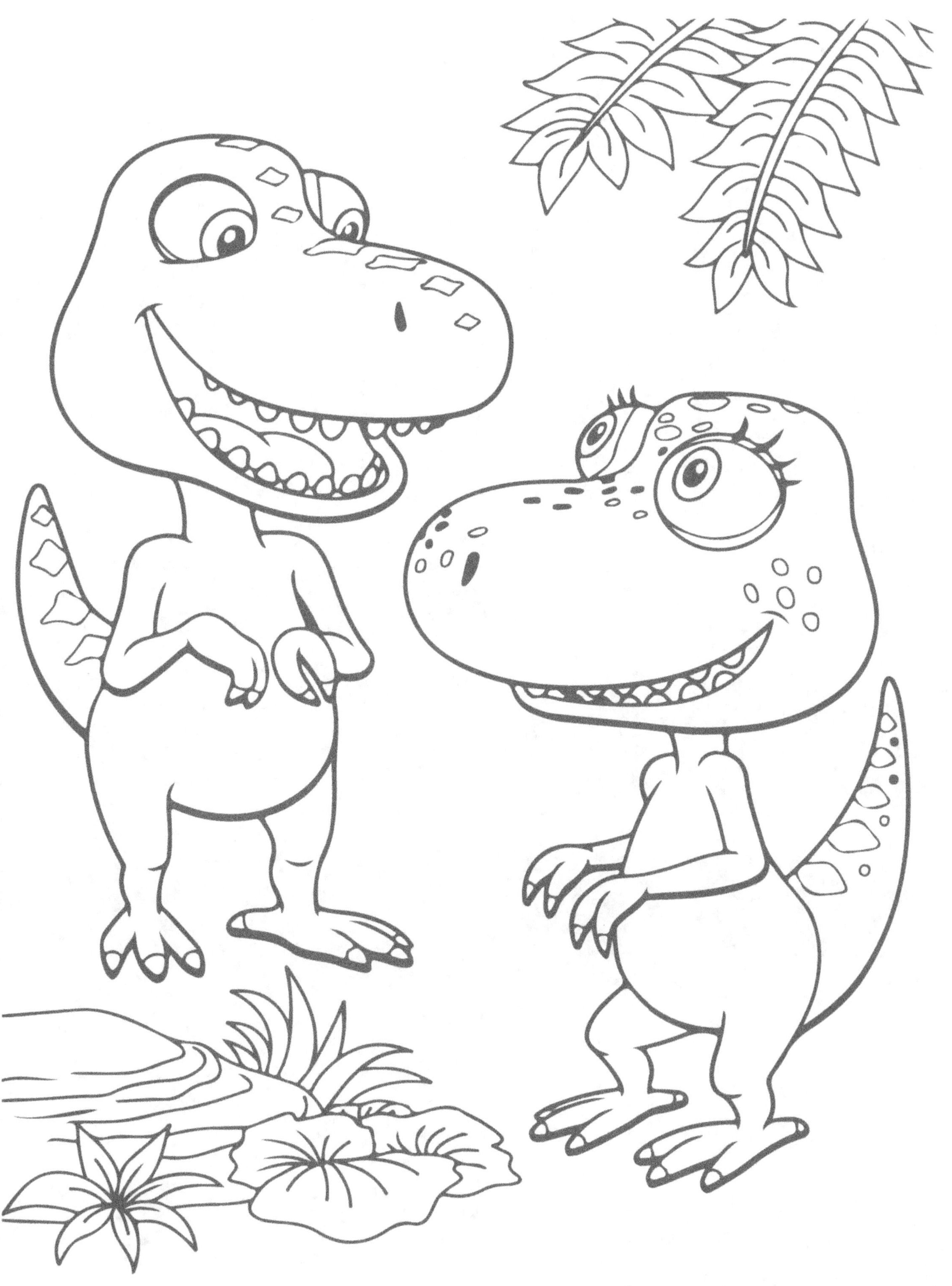

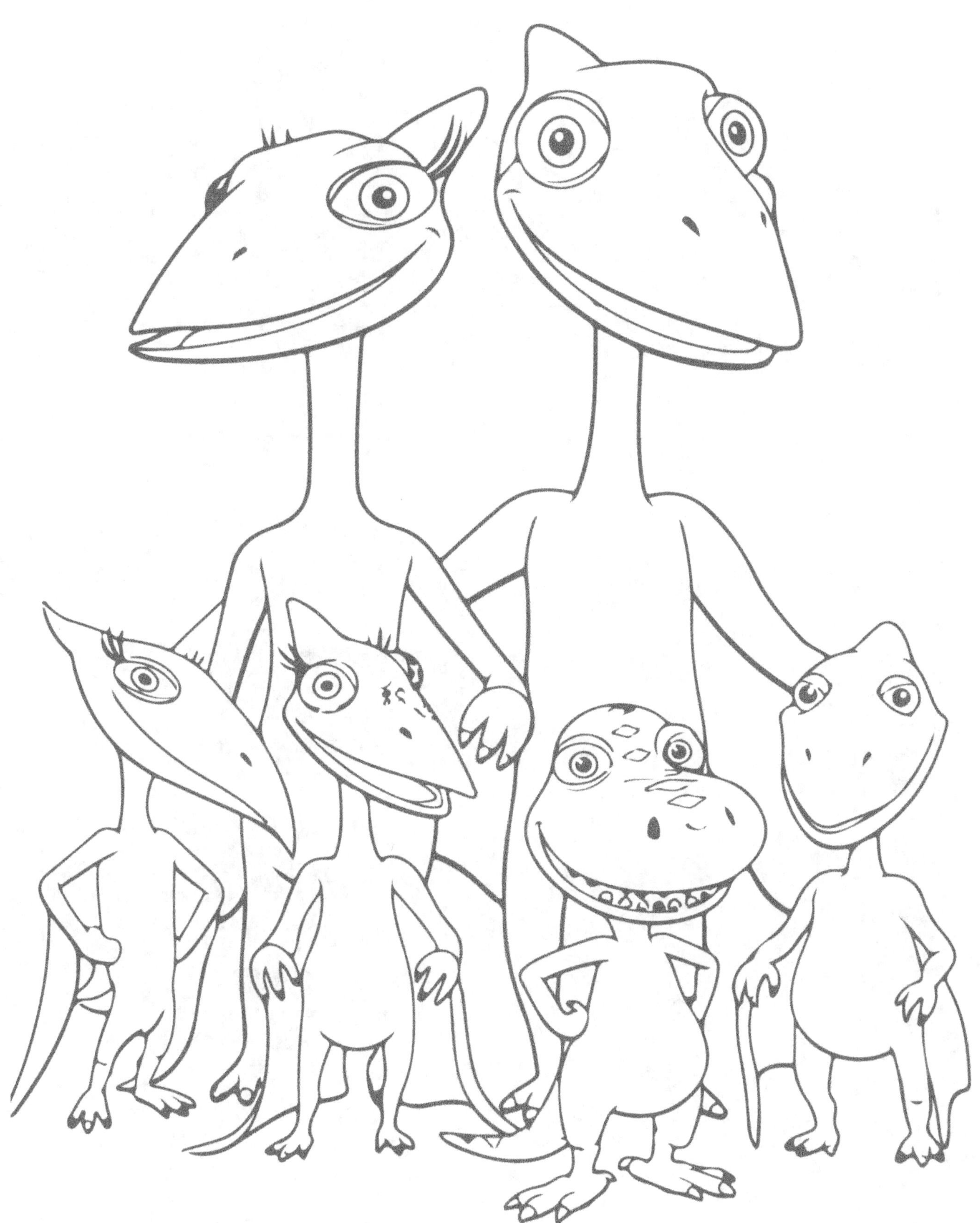

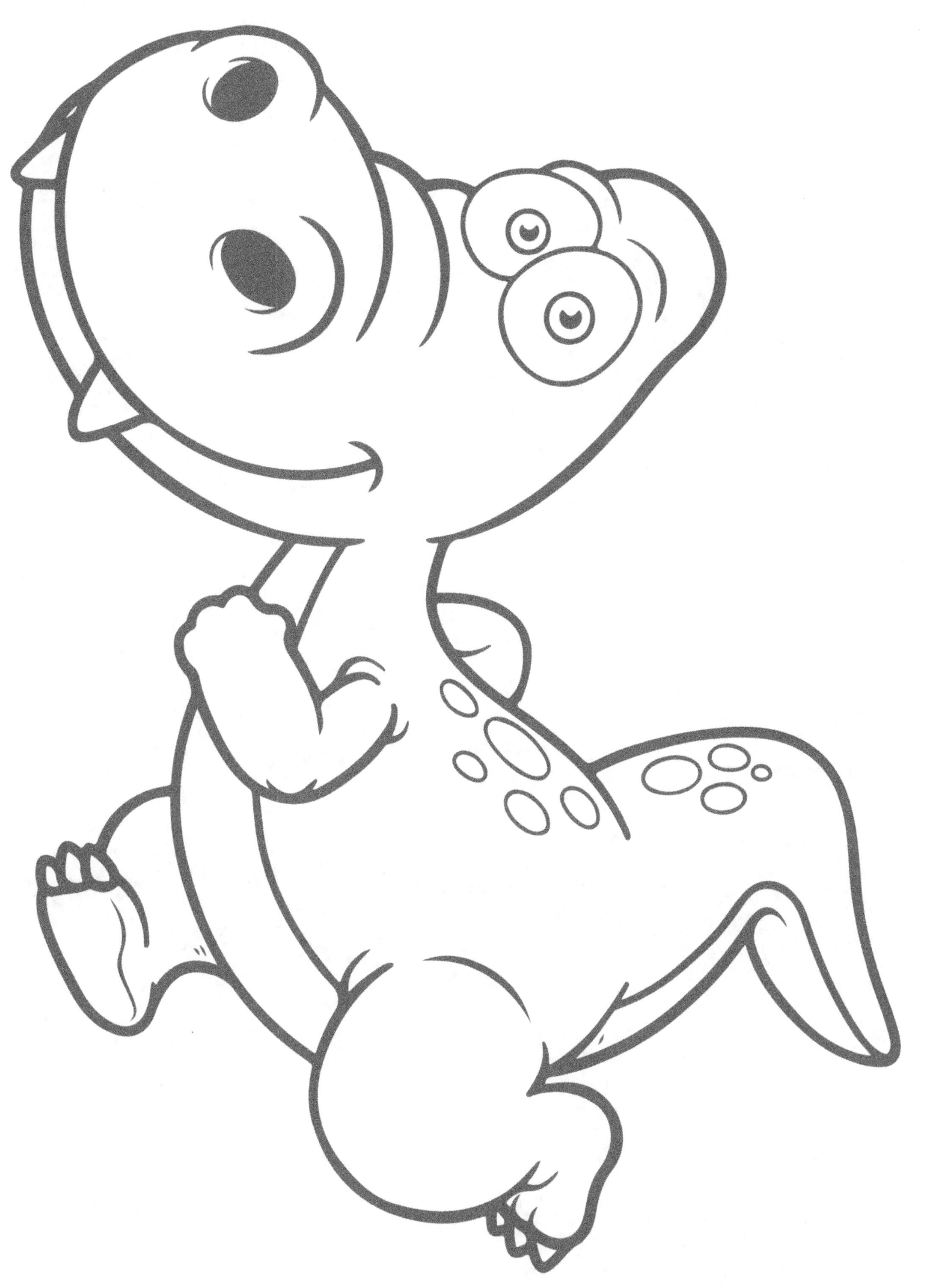

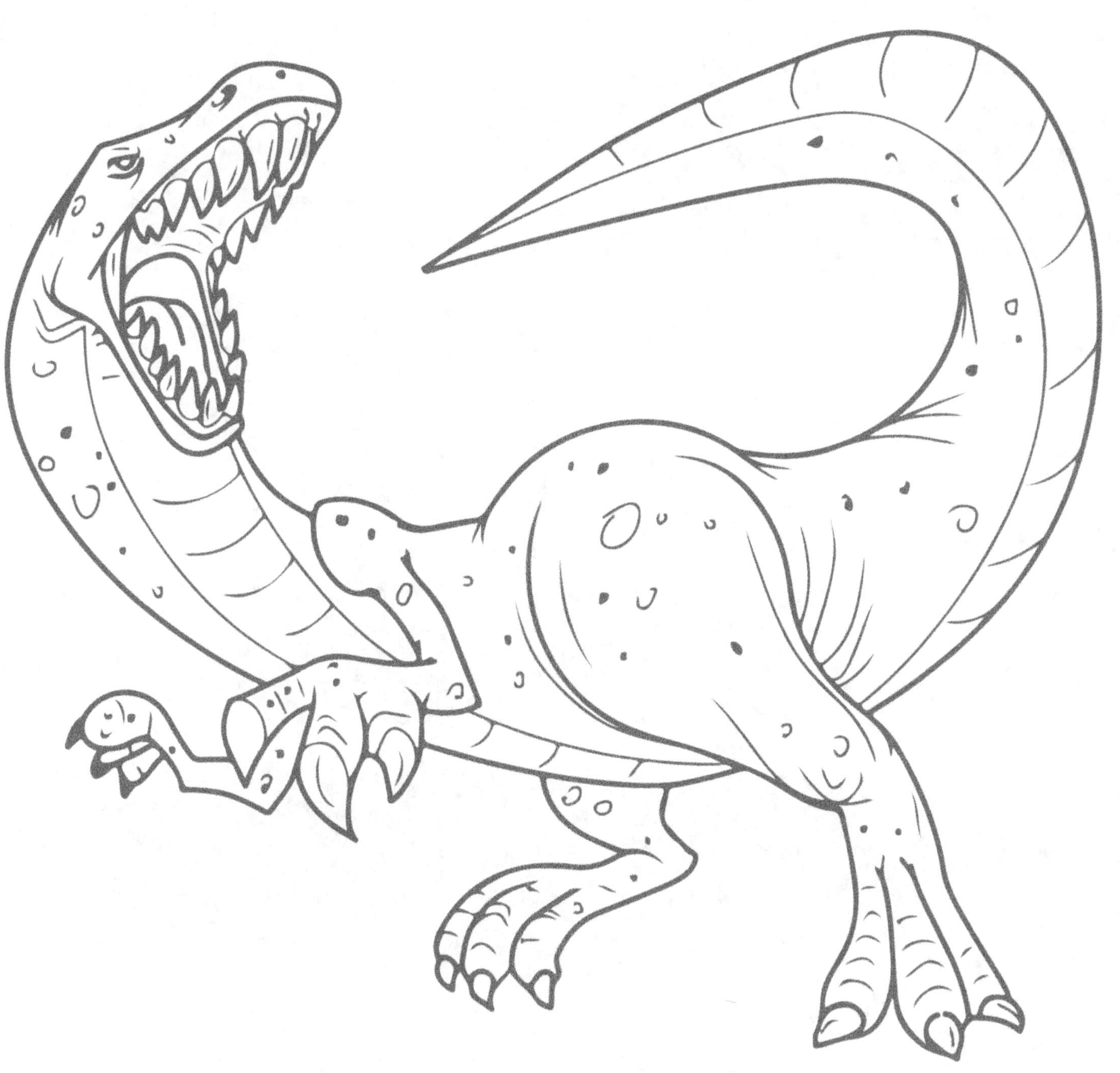

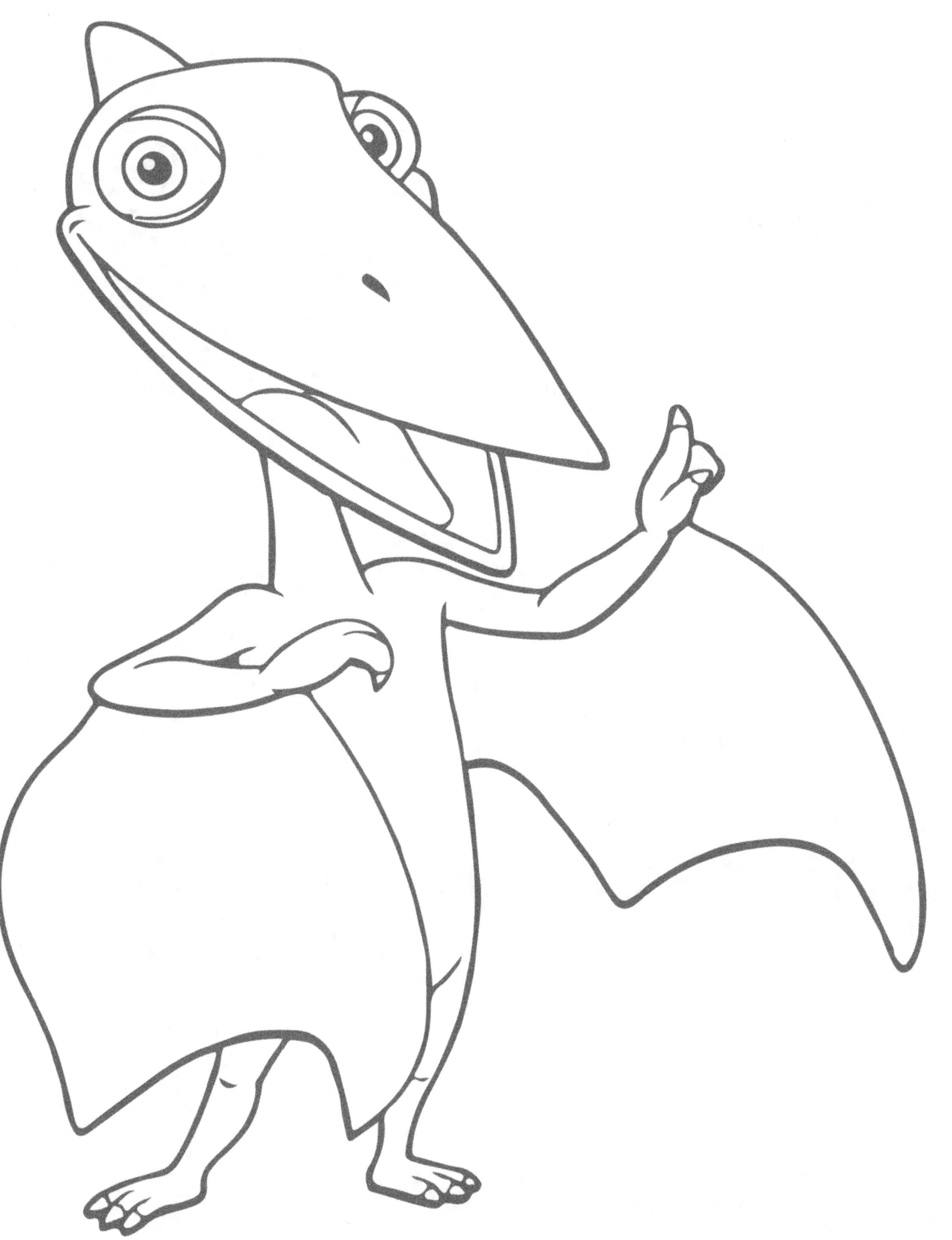

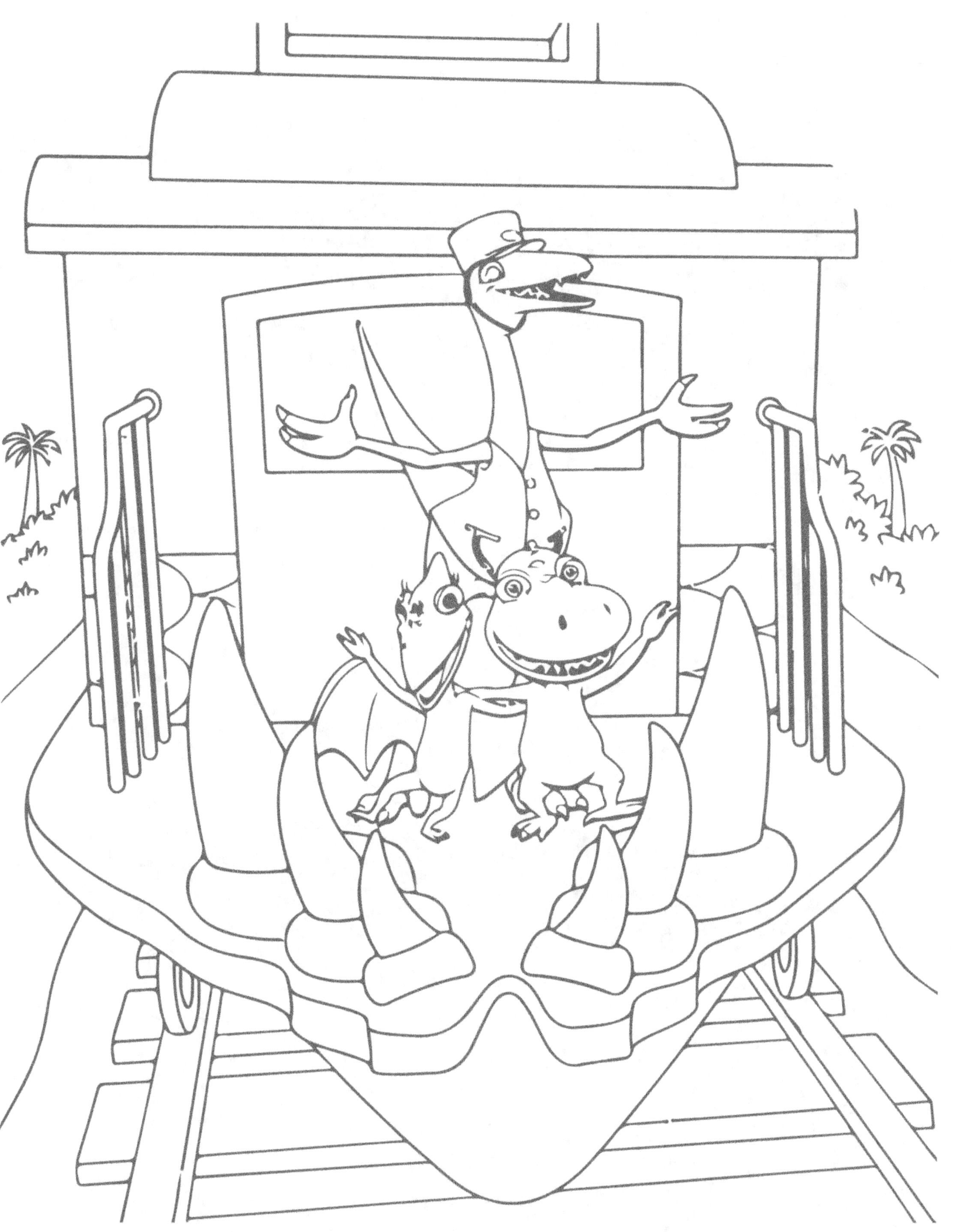

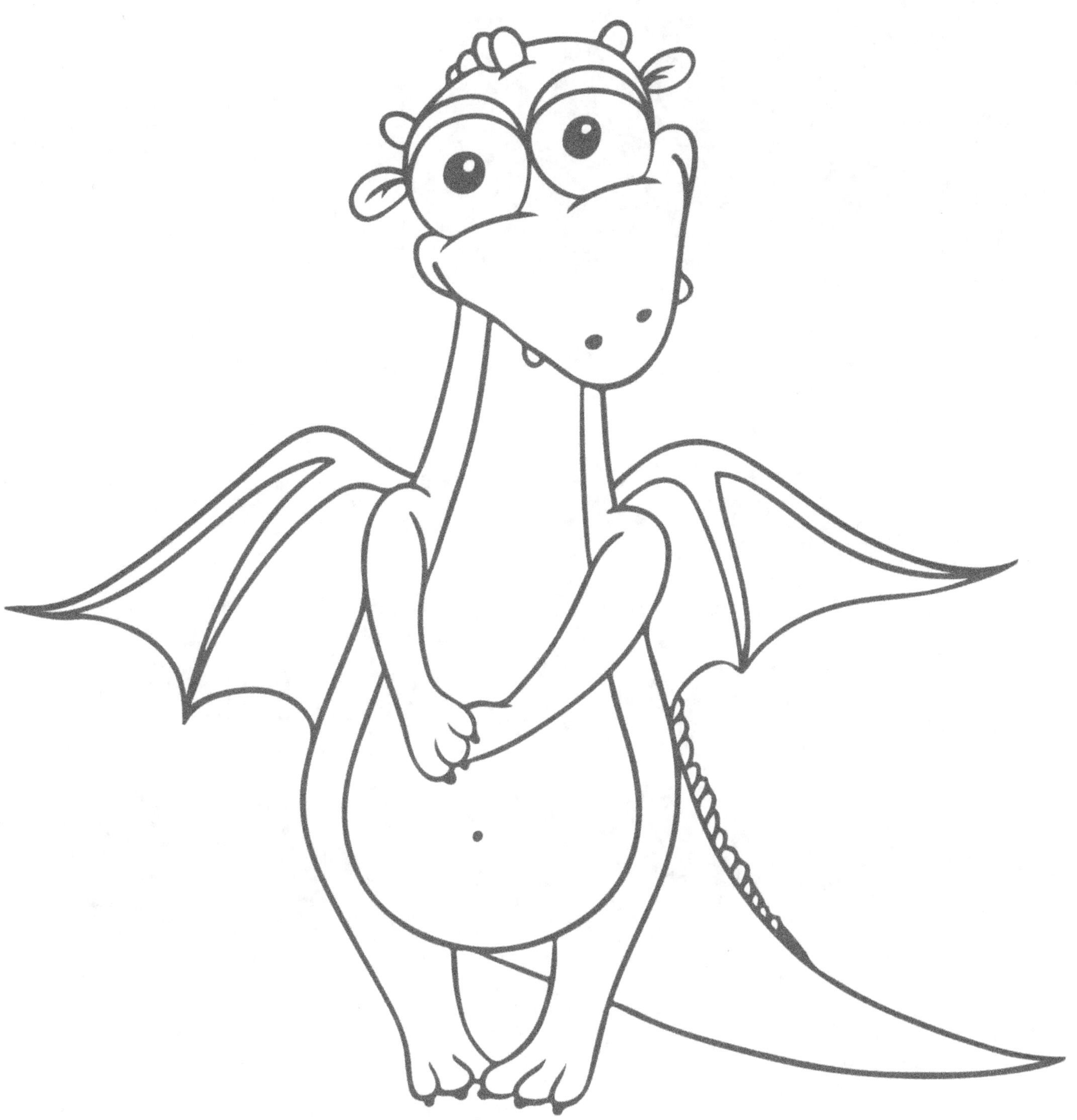

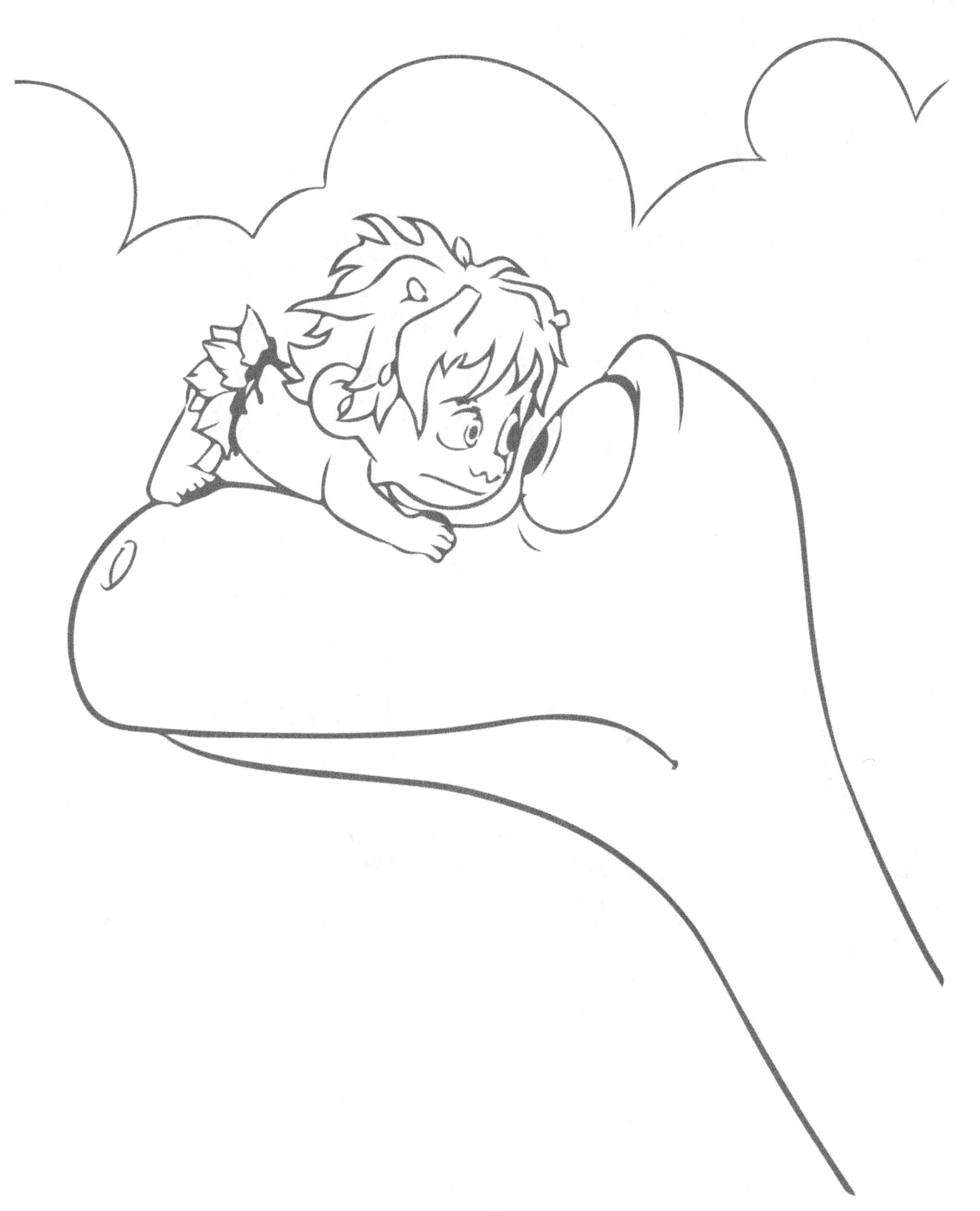

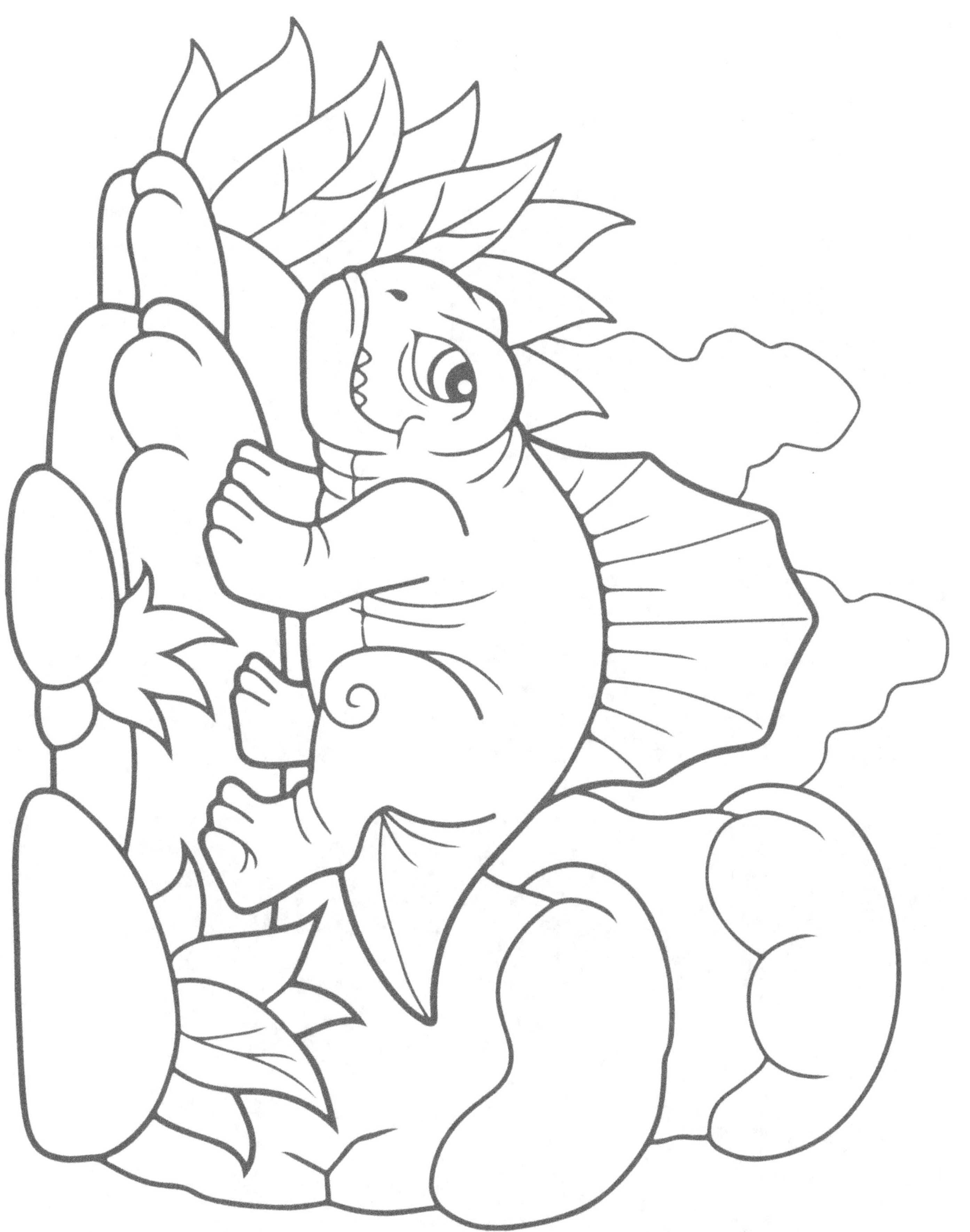

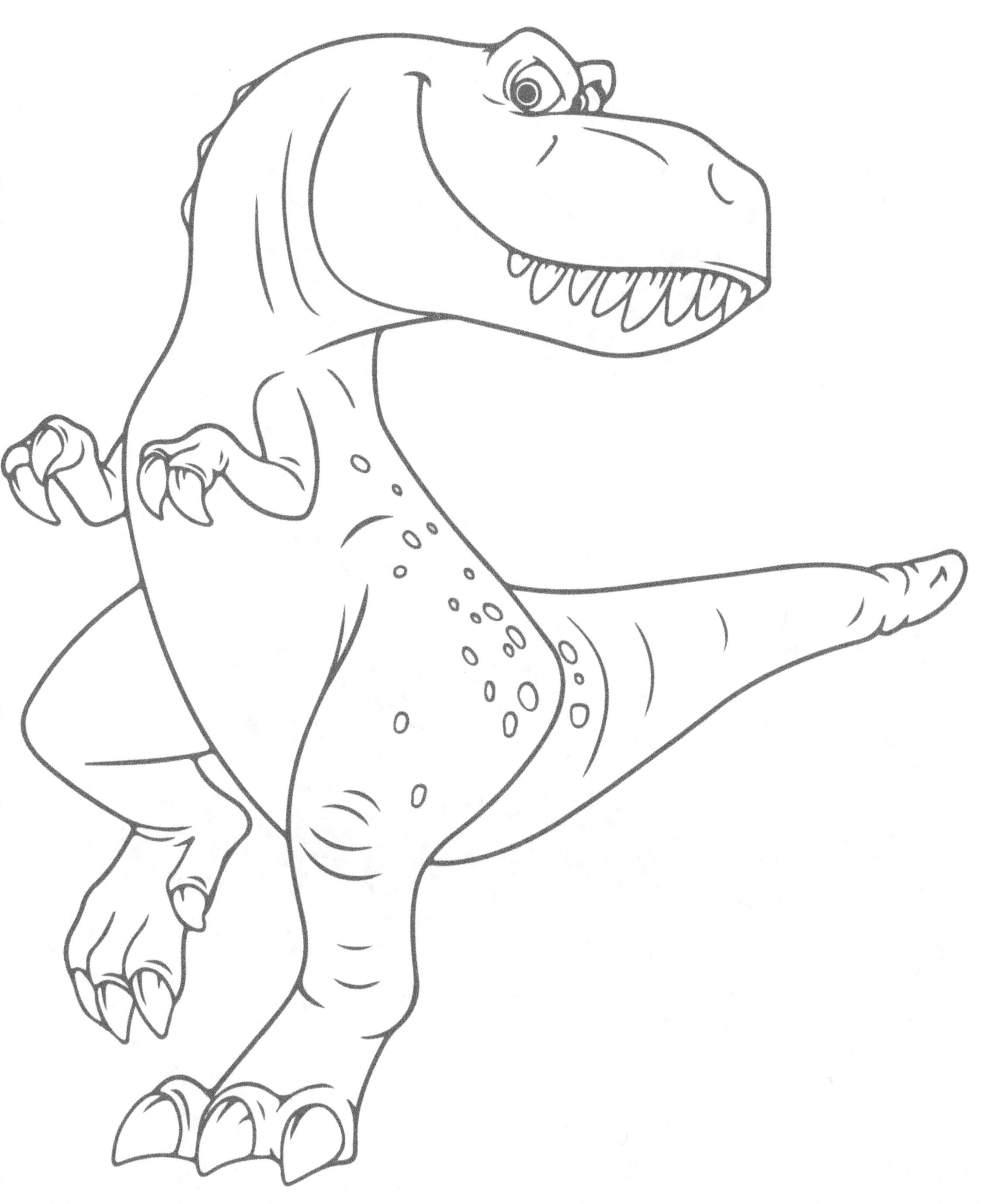

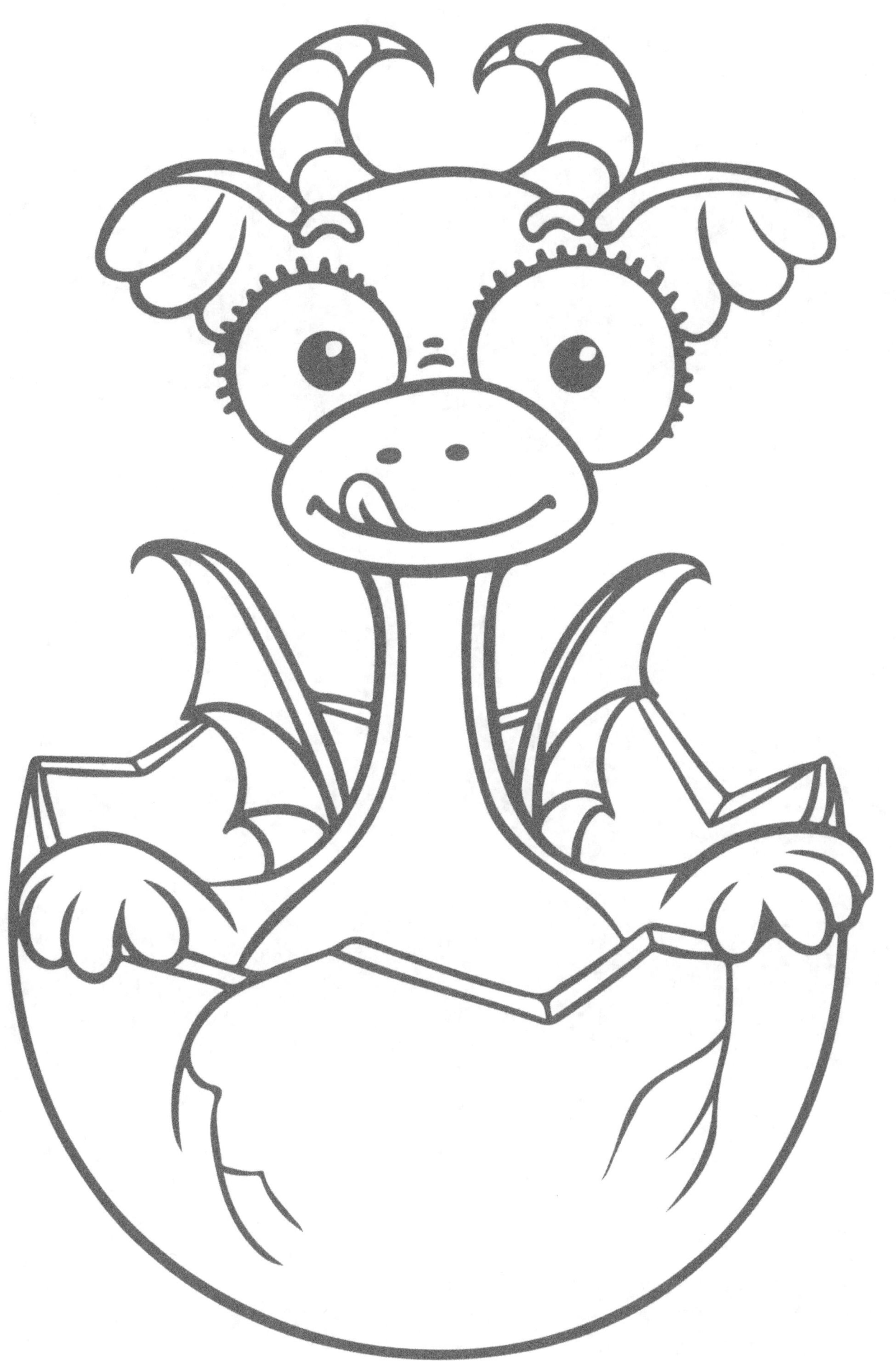

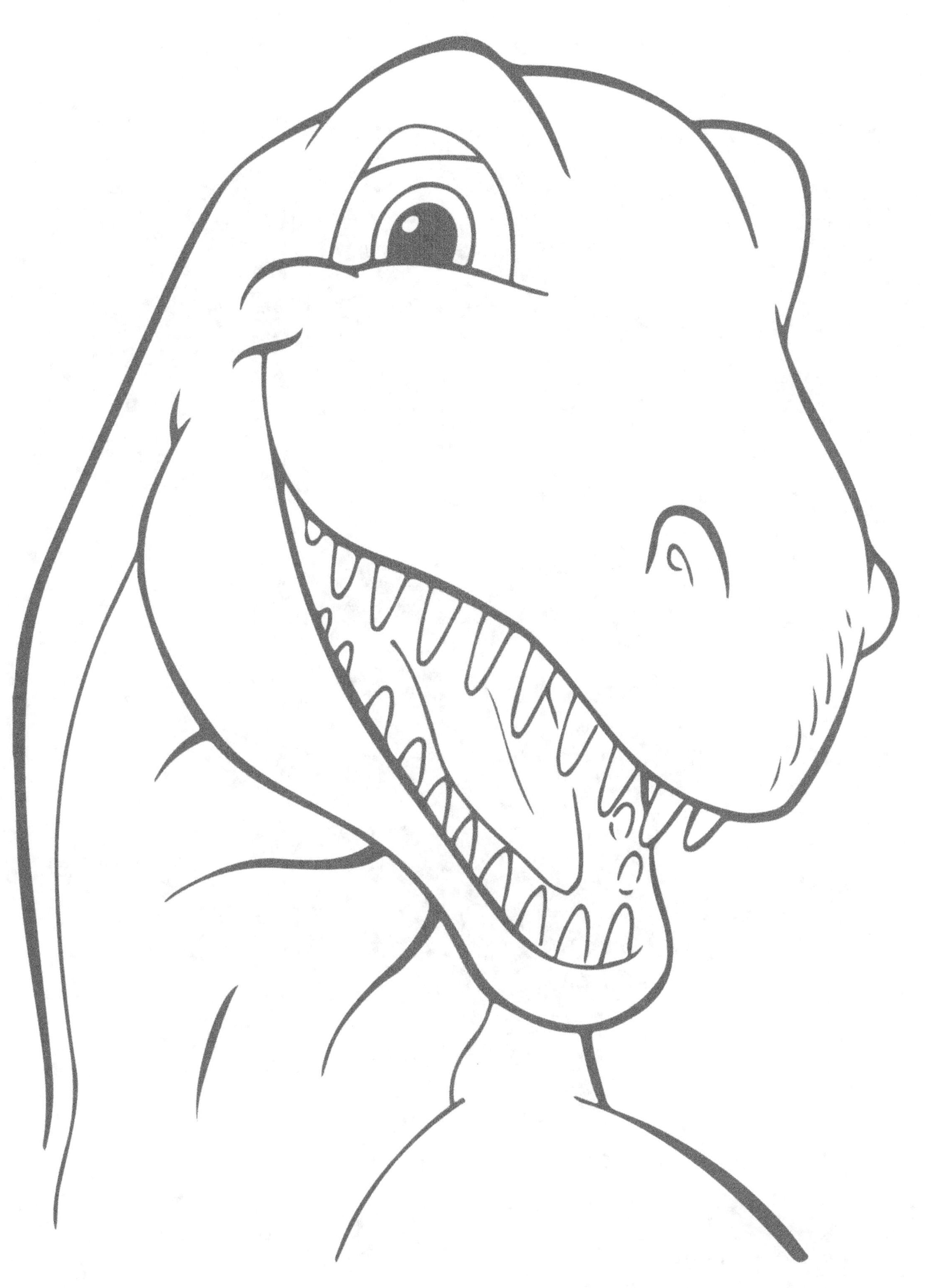

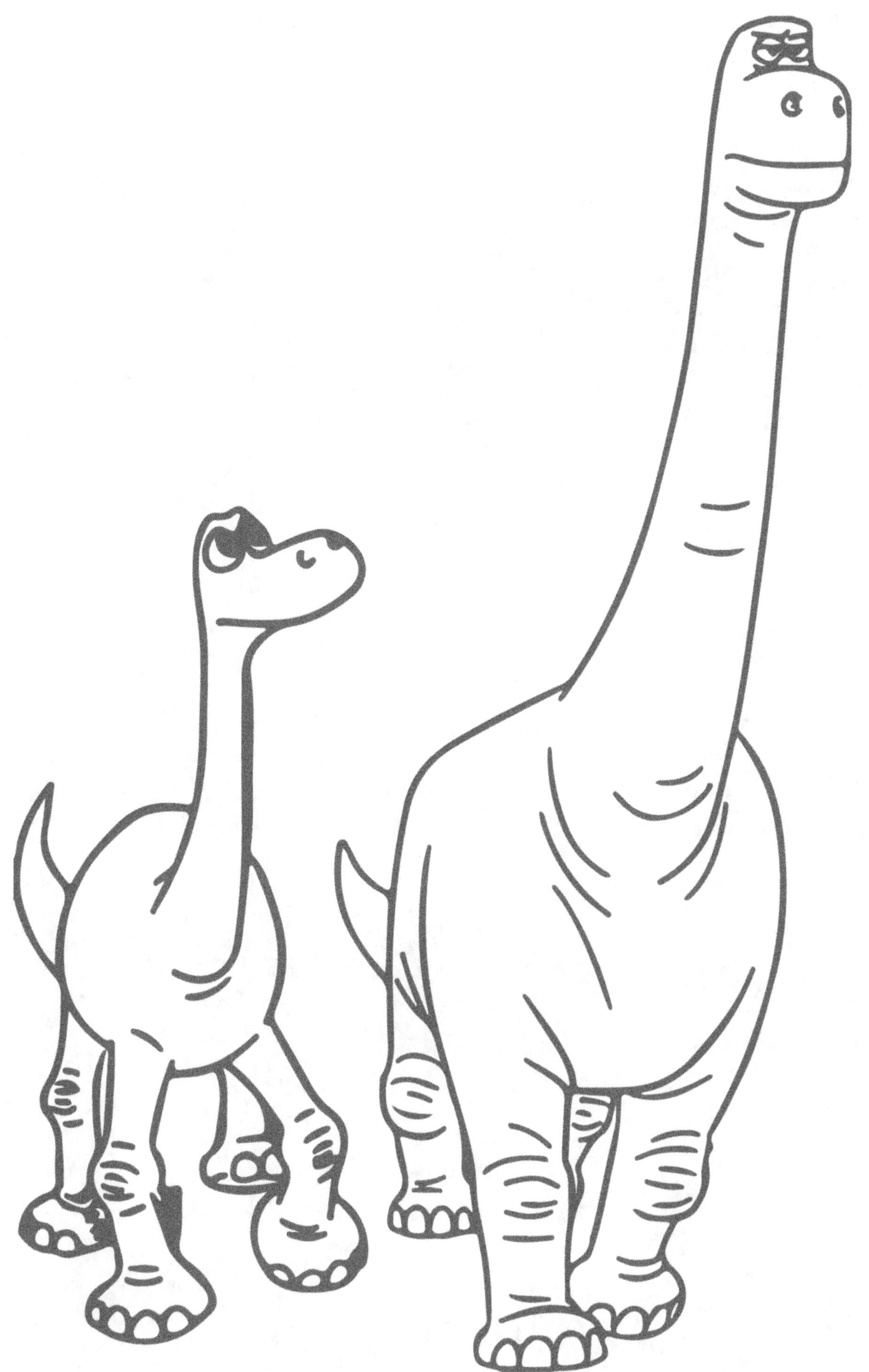

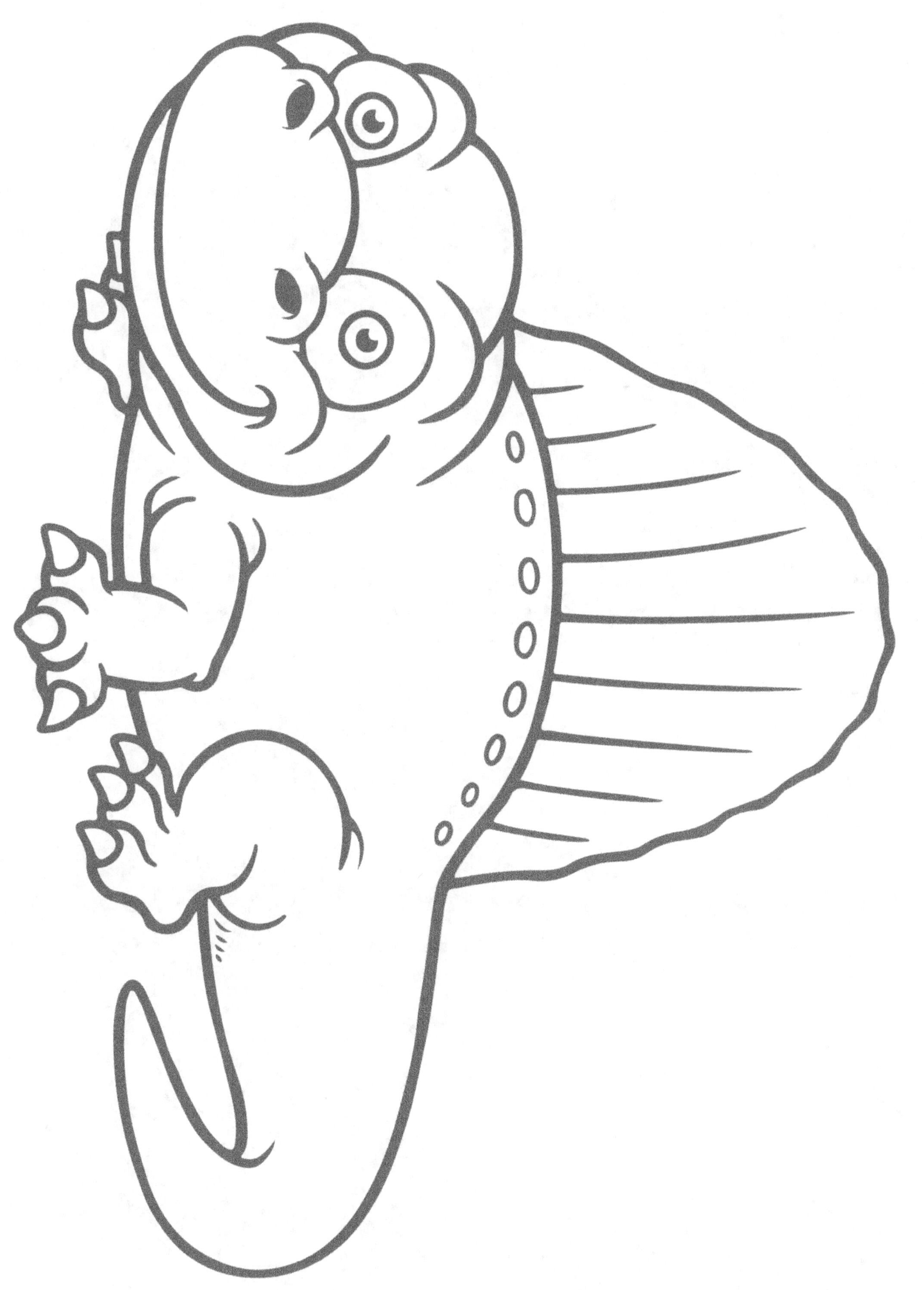

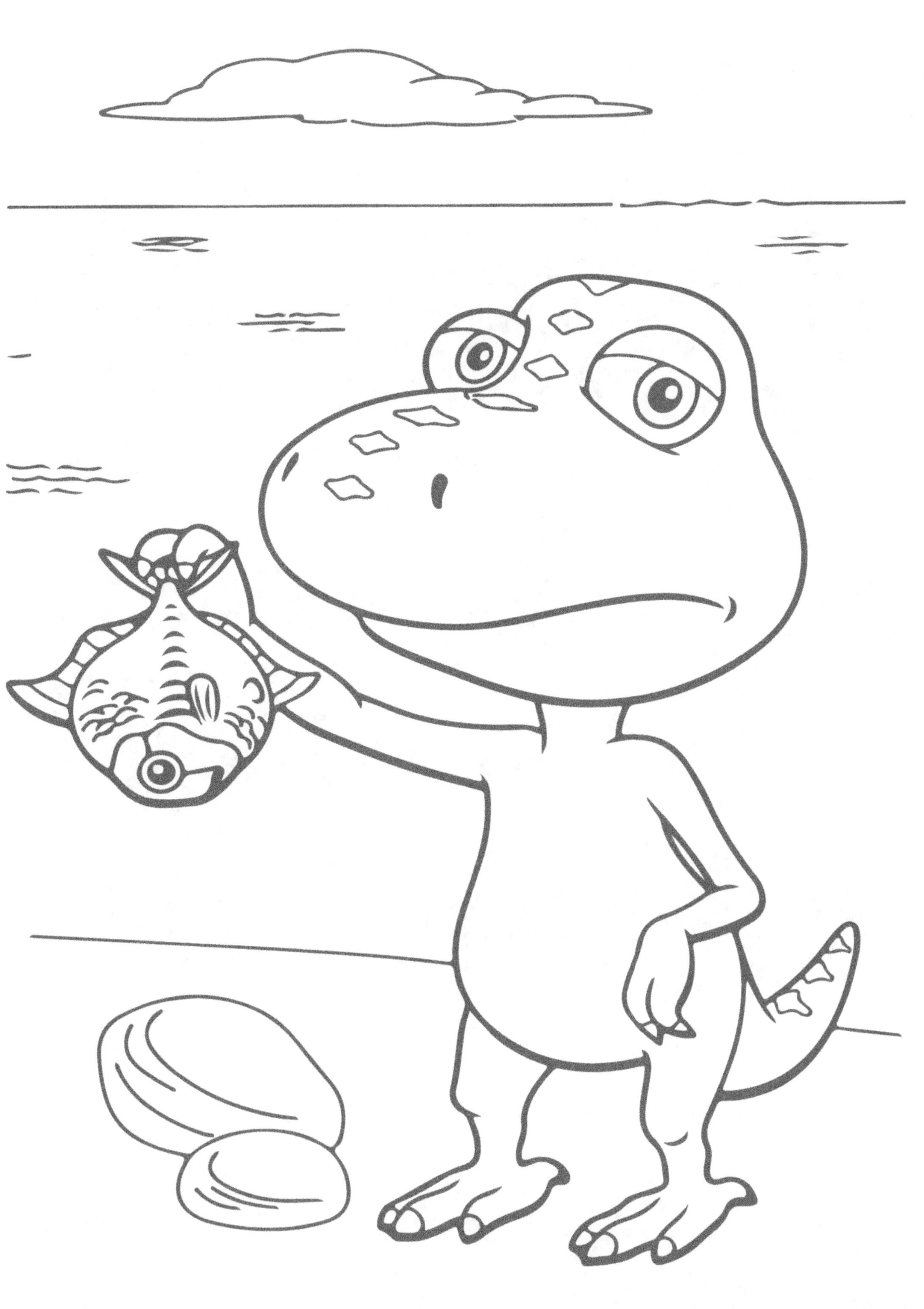

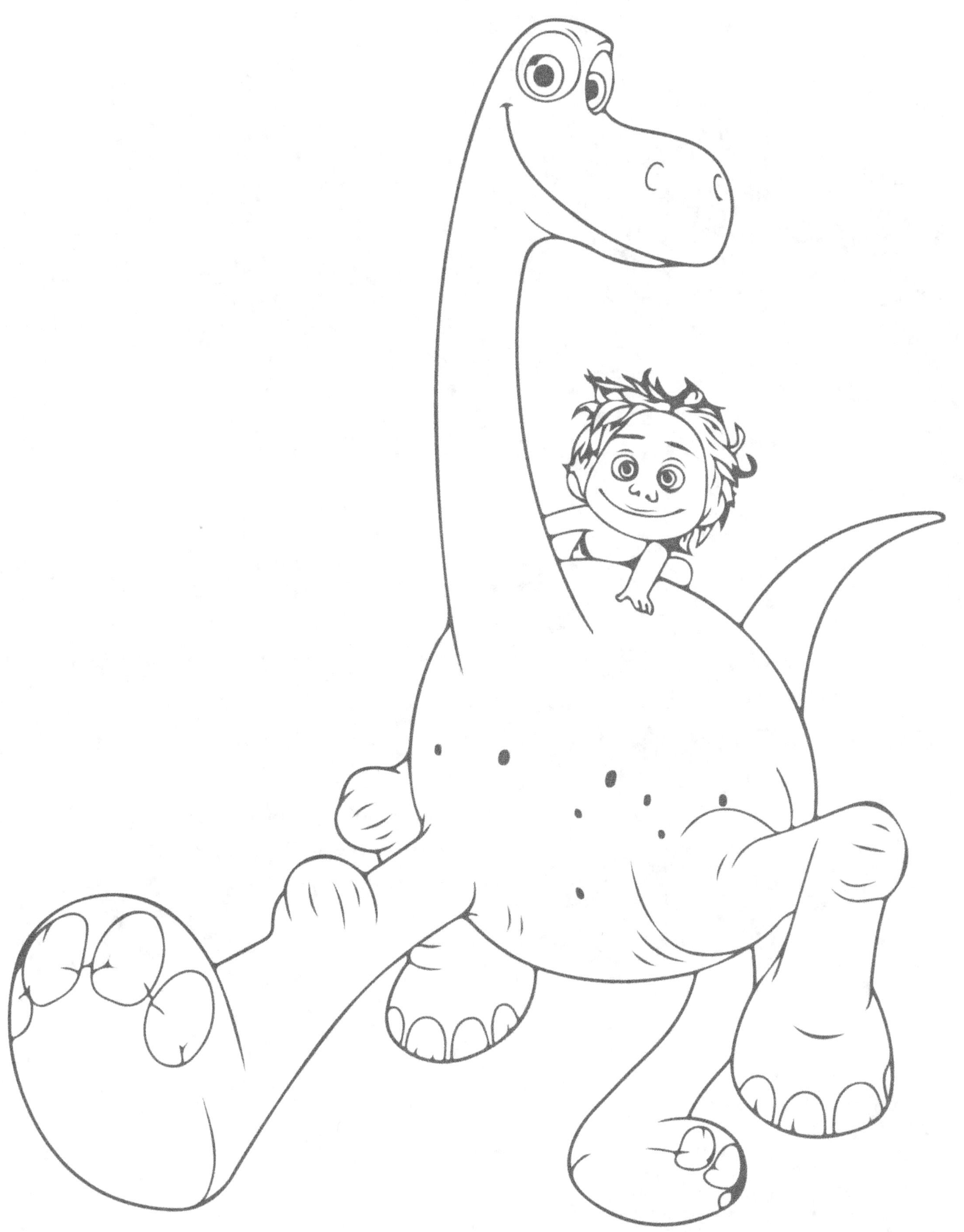

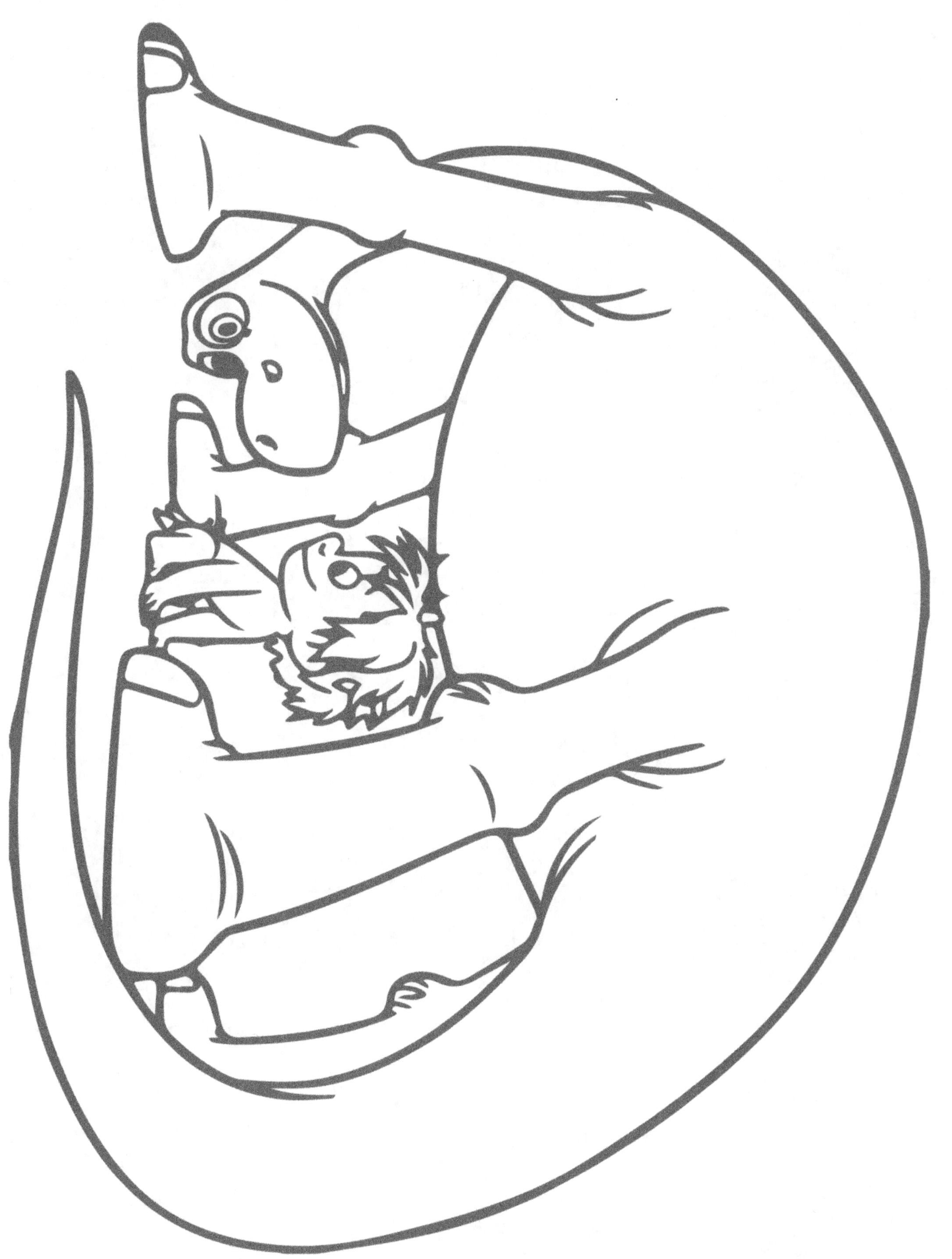

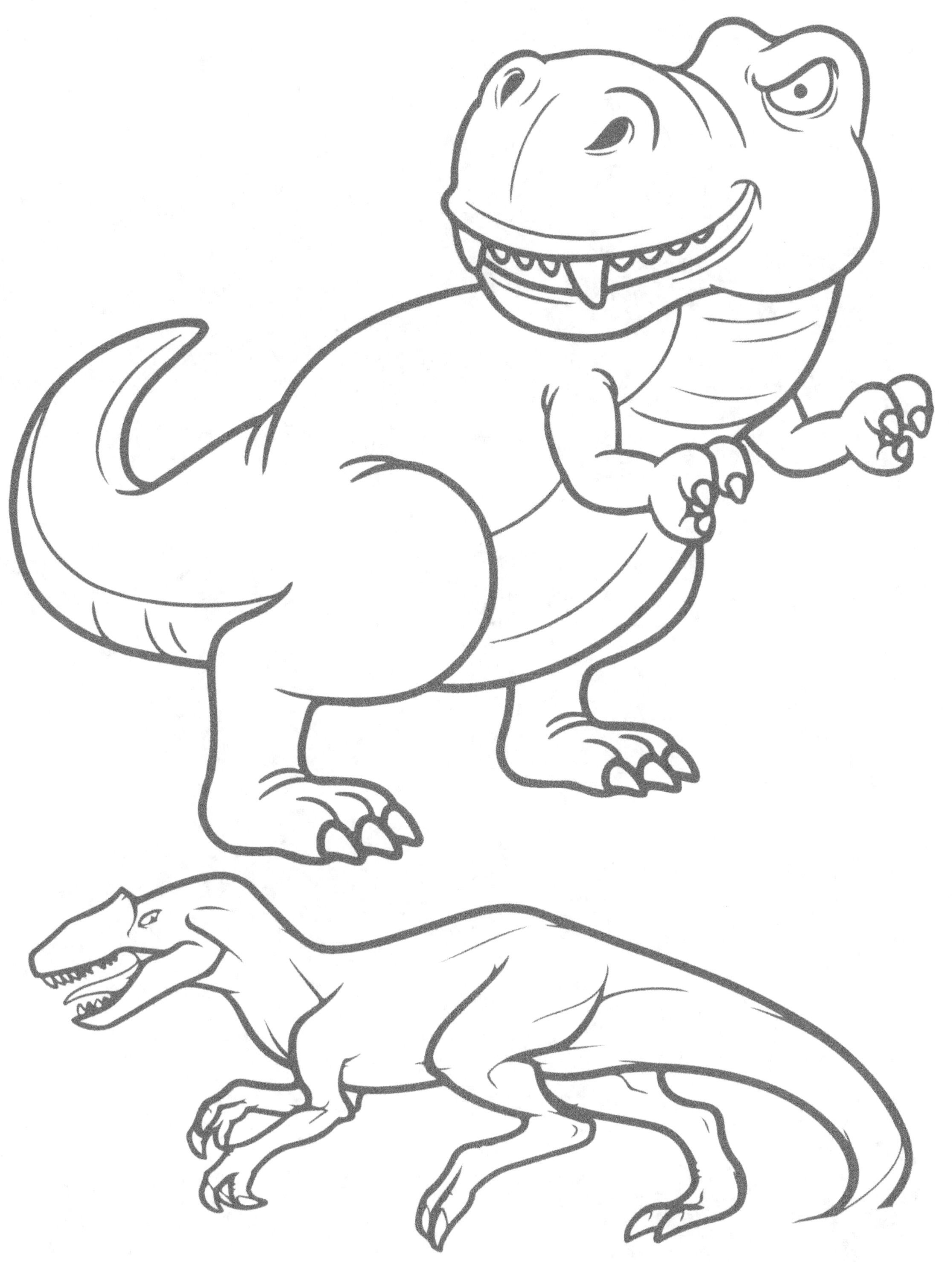

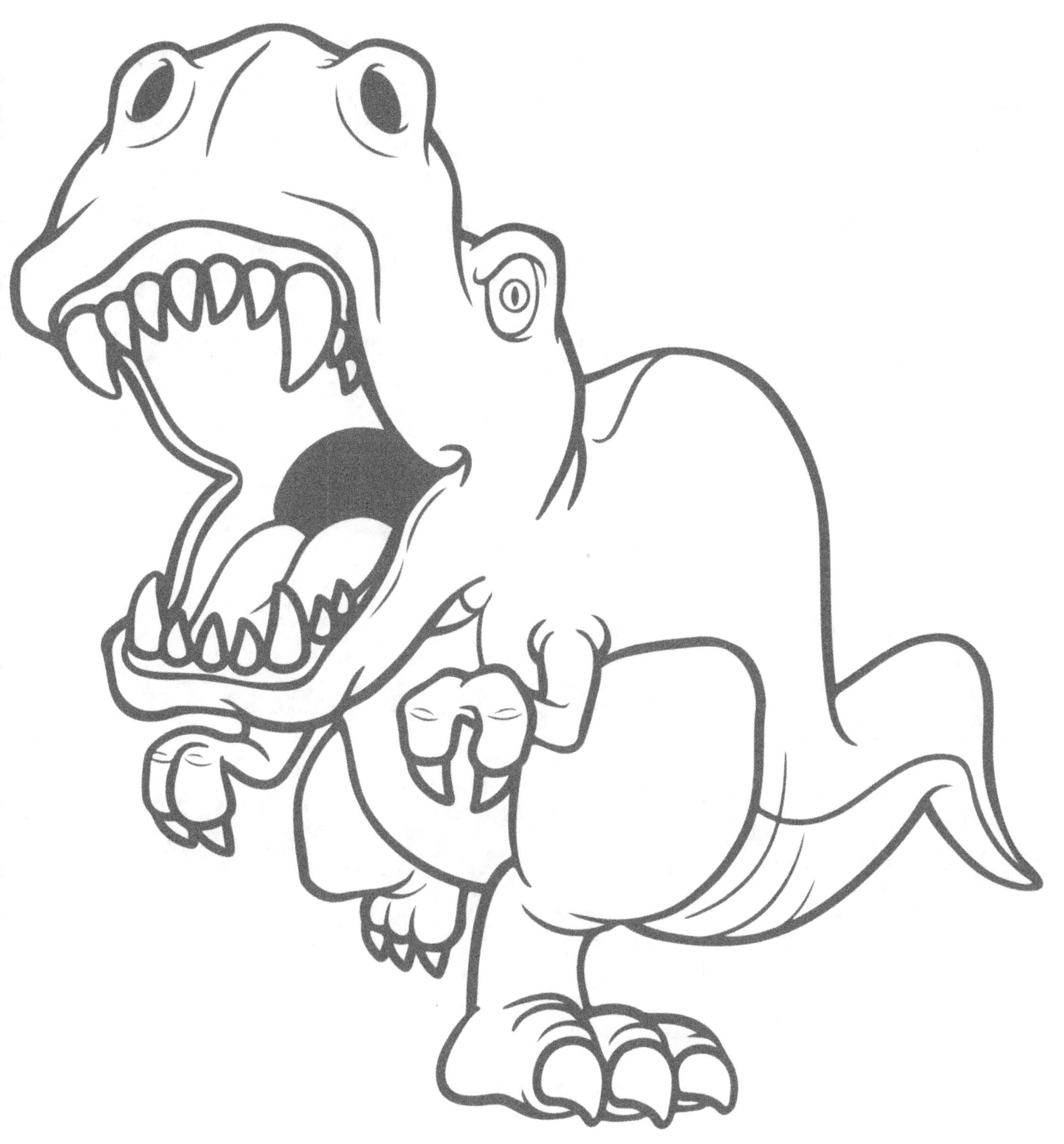

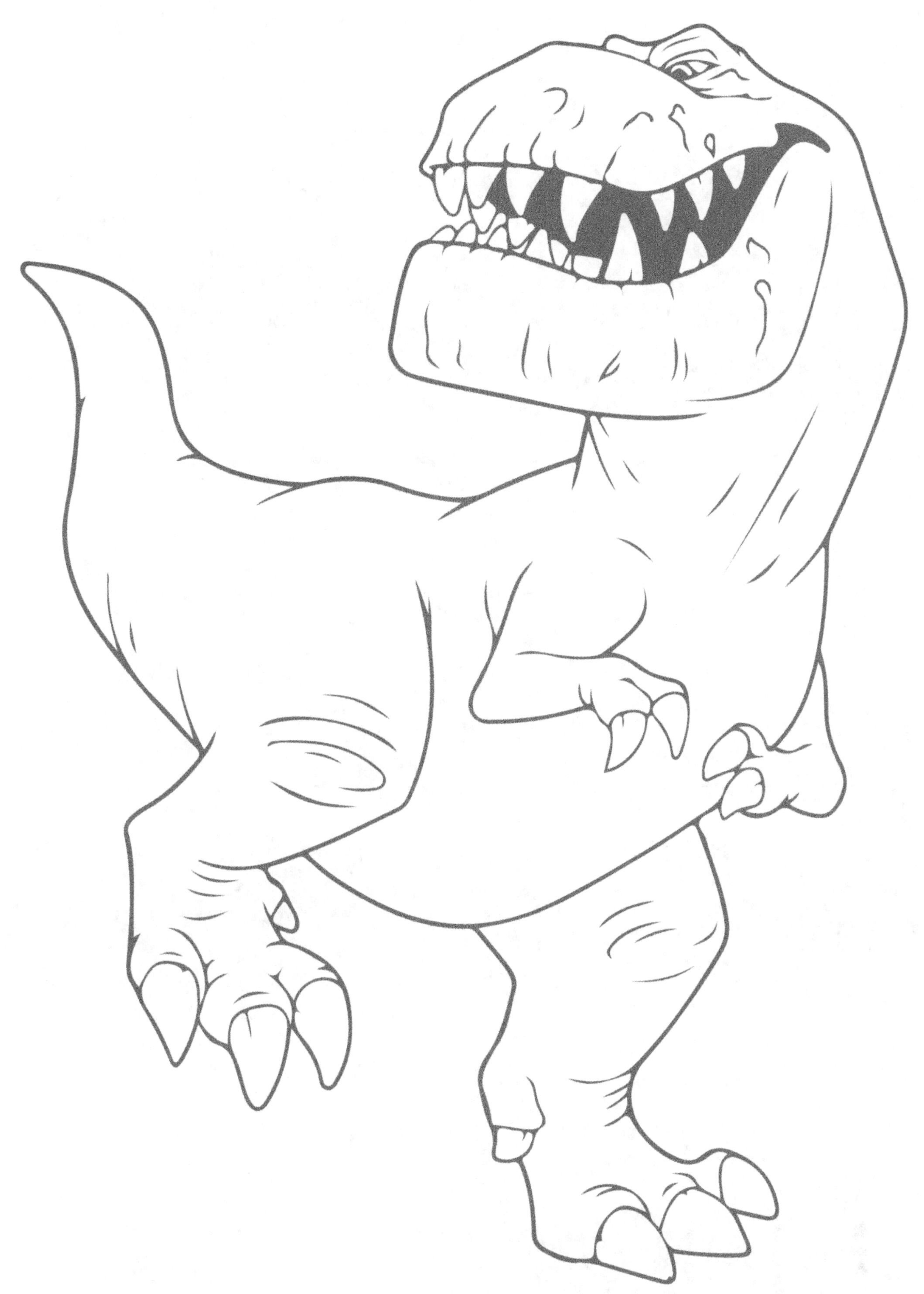

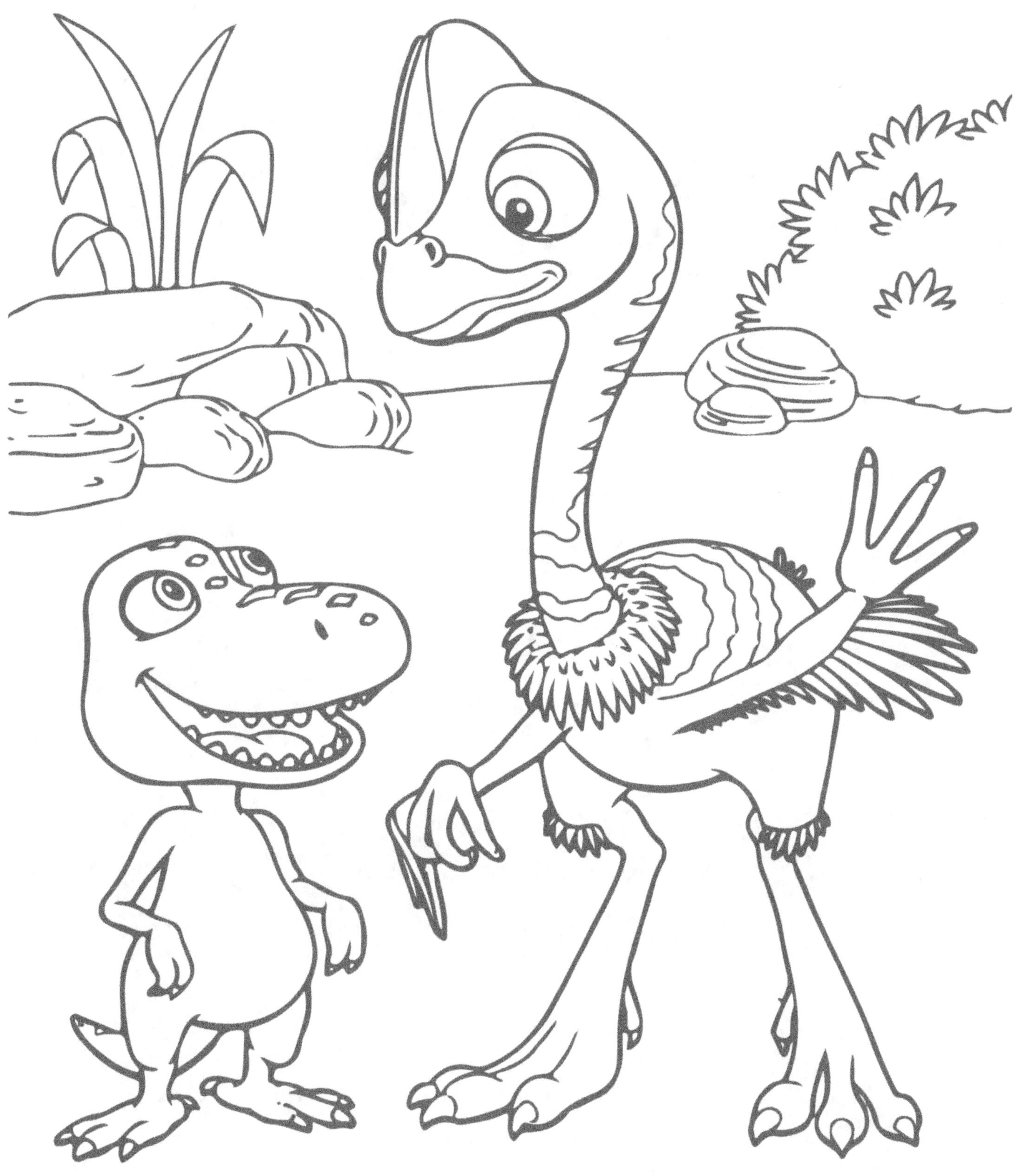